An Introduction to
The Abundance Mindset
45 Day Program

If we can simplify the process of living life and creating our circumstances, conditions, and lifestyle, it would have to be based on the notion that every decision stems from either an abundant mindset or a lack based mindset.

If you reside in the mindset of abundance, then you are also generous, calm, assured, giving, loving, never competitive, never judgmental, never envious or jealous. All of these imply you rest in a state of wholeness and completeness, this is the natural state we are born in, our natural essence.

Through living life, and the conditioning of our childhood caregivers, friends, school, and our environment, we learn limitation, doubt, fear, and most of all lack; which thereby implies shortage of time, resources, and ability. These states of being lead to jealousy, greed, competitiveness, hatred, resentment, blame, anxiety, and depression.

We are born creators! Creators of gifts that have yet to be seen, heard, or experienced. However, in order to live a life unrestricted, unbound, and unabridged we must train our mind to once again reside in the knowing, clarity, and assurance of the abundance mindset; wherein we see opportunity more often than obstacles, wherein we reside in love more often than fear, and wherein we see limitless expansion more often than doubt or restriction.

This 45 day repetitive program is designed to create new neural connections in your brain focused on gratitude, abundance, and appreciation. It further gives your mind a clear vision of your goals and visions for your desired manifestations.

You will notice a shift in your thinking and emotions, thereby a shift in your perception of your life circumstances. You will also start to notice more opportunities presented and a shift in your overall energy patterns. In the process of creating your new and desired life, you will thereby experience a new state of being as a natural consequence of the shift in your thoughts, emotions, and overall personality which creates your personal reality.

You deserve to live the life of your dreams. Never miss a day in the creation of your desired future life.

I wish for you a life lived in love, happiness and immense abundance.

With Gratitude,

Milan Consi

THE ABUNDANCE JOURNAL
The "HOW TO" 45 Day Program in Creating a Mindset of Abundance BY: MILAN CONSI

STEP 1 - FINDING STILLNESS
Connecting with PRESENT MOMENT AWARENESS (PMA)
1. Go Within - close your eyes and find the stillness.
2. Listen - activate your auditory sense and take notice of the sounds around you.
3. Connect With The Body - feel the touch of your fingers on your skin.
4. Become Grounded - feel your body as it becomes grounded in the PMA.
5. Breathe - take 3 deep breaths and release.

STEP 2 - WHAT & WHO BRINGS YOU LOVE
1. Connect and place your attention on the heart.
2. List 5 people or things that make you feel love or be loved.
3. Put your hand on your heart and FEEL the LOVE in the PMA.

STEP 3 - JAR OF GOOD THINGS
1. As you awaken, write down something good, past or present.
2. Mid-day, write down something good, past or present.
3. Before you sleep, write down something good, past or present.
4. Take a few moments and FEEL the GRATITUDE in the PMA.

STEP 4 - FUTURE GOALS AND VISIONS

1. Write 3 goals or visions you wish to manifest during the following 6 to 12 months.
2. Next to the goal, write the EMOTION you would experience once you had manifested your desired goal/vision.
3. Take a few moments and FEEL the EMOTIONS in the PMA.

STEP 5 - BECOMING THE IDEAL VERSION OF YOURSELF, your own HERO.

1. Write down the characteristics of the future YOU that has accomplished your goals.
2. How would your future self walk, talk, carry themselves, and live their dream life?
3. What would your life look life, who would be in your life?
4. What would be the dominant EMOTIONS of your future HERO SELF?
5. Take a few moments and FEEL the EMOTIONS in the PMA.

LIST OF AFFIRMATIONS AND MY TRUTHS

I AM Divine

I AM Loved

I AM Adored

I AM Protected

I AM Free

I AM Abundant

I AM Successful

I AM Wealthy

I AM Healthy

I AM Prosperous

I AM Beautiful

I AM Youthful

I AM ONE with the SOURCE within me.

I AM in the receptive flow of the GOODNESS of the Universe.

I AM Love

I AM Blessed

I BLESS and PROSPER everyone and everything, and everyone and everything blesses and prospers me.

The Universe is the only SOURCE of my supply.

Abundance is my BIRTHRIGHT.

I was born to THRIVE, and will always THRIVE.

I LIVE WELL each day of my life.

The Universe ALWAYS has my back.

Success is the ONLY TRUE mechanism of the the Universe, and therefore, all of its creations. My life gets BETTER and BETTER each and every day.

I expect the BEST and ONLY THE BEST comes to me.

We are all here to help each other GROW, PROSPER, and LOVE.

I am DIVINELY guided each and every day, in each and every way.

I have a GRATEFUL HEART.

Everything comes to me in PERFECT TIMING and PERFECT FLOW.

I am a MONEY MAGNET.

SUCCESS is always chasing me.

I have PERFECT HEALTH.

YOUTH is my TRUE ESSENCE.

Each step I take magnifies my SUCCESS.

Each breath I take magnifies my ABUNDANCE.

Each blink of my eyes solidifies my connection with SOURCE.

EVERYTHING is always working out for me.

I can DO, BE, and HAVE everything I DESIRE.

I am POWERFUL beyond measure.

Life is meant to be FUN and AMAZING.

The UNIVERSE always provides in PERFECT TIMING and PERFECT FLOW.

I CONNECT with the frequency of WEALTH.

I am ASTONISHINGLY ABUNDANT.

I am a person that experiences CONSTANT and CONTINUOUS WEALTH.

I am always INSPIRING and INFLUENCING others to CONNECT to their STREAM OF WEALTH.

I am a CREATOR, inspired by UNIVERSAL forces to flow in accordance to my DREAMS and DESIRES.

FOREVER massive ABUNDANCE is my daily experience.

I am a person that lives in tremendous GRATITUDE.

As the sun rises and pours its WEALTH upon the Earth, so too does ABUNDANCE pour its WEALTH onto me.

I am a MASTER MANIFESTOR.

I love SHARING my ABUNDANCE with others.

I know that the flow of ABUNDANCE is never ending.

I am KIND, WEALTHY, GIVING, SPIRITUAL, and continually EVOLVING.

I am UNLIMITED in my expression of creativity in this world.

I am WIDE OPEN to all kinds of ABUNDANCE from the Universe.

I have vast OPPORTUNITIES as INSPIRATION continues to flow through me.

I have the CONFIDENCE to TRUST the FLOW of guidance that I receive.

I am HUMBLE in my ABUNDANCE.

I am PROFOUNDLY PROSPEROUS.

I am ENTIRELY ABUNDANT.

I have found what I LOVE to CREATE and now money flows easily into my life.

I follow my INSPIRATION and PASSION, thereby allowing the natural flow of ABUNDANCE. I TRUST in PERFECT TIMING and PERFECT FLOW.

I am LIVING my DREAM LIFE right NOW.

I am CREATING my ABUNDANCE with each positive thought.

I am VALUED by the Universe as my thoughts ALIGN with the SOURCE that radiates LIFE, LOVE and ABUNDANCE.

I reward others and bring value to their lives by becoming the MOST ABUNDANT version of myself.

I am MEANT to LIVE WELL and THRIVE.

I am MEANT to LIVE in JOY and PROSPERITY.

I am MEANT to INSPIRE and ELEVATE others in my own REALIZATION of my ALIGNMENT with SOURCE.

These are meant to be sample affirmations and truths. Feel free to create your own as they resonate with your own being.

DAY_____ OF THE 45 DAY ABUNDANCE MINDSET ACTIVATION

WHAT ARE YOUR TRUTHS?

CONFIDENTLY state your truths and affirmations today.

I AM _____

I AM _____

I AM _____

STEP 2 - WHAT & WHO BRINGS YOU LOVE

1. _____

2. _____

3. _____

4. _____

5. _____

STEP 3 - JAR OF GOOD THINGS

1. SUNRISE_____

2. MID-DAY_____

3. SUNSET _____

STEP 4 - FUTURE GOALS & VISIONS

1. _____ DESIRED EMOTION _____

2. _____ DESIRED EMOTION _____

3. _____ DESIRED EMOTION _____

STEP 5 - BECOMING YOUR IDEAL VERSION, your own HERO

Who will you be: _____

What title will you hold: _____

Who will be in your life: _____

What will your life look like:_____

What emotions will you mainly embody: _____

DAY_____ OF THE 45 DAY ABUNDANCE MINDSET ACTIVATION

WHAT ARE YOUR TRUTHS?

CONFIDENTLY state your truths and affirmations today.

I AM _____

I AM _____

I AM _____

STEP 2 - WHAT & WHO BRINGS YOU LOVE

1. _____

2. _____

3. _____

4. _____

5. _____

STEP 3 - JAR OF GOOD THINGS

1. SUNRISE_____

2. MID-DAY_____

3. SUNSET _____

STEP 4 - FUTURE GOALS & VISIONS

1. _____ DESIRED EMOTION _____

2. _____ DESIRED EMOTION _____

3. _____ DESIRED EMOTION _____

STEP 5 - BECOMING YOUR IDEAL VERSION, your own HERO

Who will you be: _____

What title will you hold: _____

Who will be in your life: _____

What will your life look like:_____

What emotions will you mainly embody: _____

DAY_____ OF THE 45 DAY ABUNDANCE MINDSET ACTIVATION

WHAT ARE YOUR TRUTHS?

CONFIDENTLY state your truths and affirmations today.

I AM _____

I AM _____

I AM _____

STEP 2 - WHAT & WHO BRINGS YOU LOVE

1. _____

2. _____

3. _____

4. _____

5. _____

STEP 3 - JAR OF GOOD THINGS

1. SUNRISE_____

2. MID-DAY_____

3. SUNSET _____

STEP 4 - FUTURE GOALS & VISIONS

1. _____ DESIRED EMOTION _____

2. _____ DESIRED EMOTION _____

3. _____ DESIRED EMOTION _____

STEP 5 - BECOMING YOUR IDEAL VERSION, your own HERO

Who will you be: _____

What title will you hold: _____

Who will be in your life: _____

What will your life look like:_____

What emotions will you mainly embody: _____

DAY_____ OF THE 45 DAY ABUNDANCE MINDSET ACTIVATION

WHAT ARE YOUR TRUTHS?

CONFIDENTLY state your truths and affirmations today.

I AM _____

I AM _____

I AM _____

STEP 2 - WHAT & WHO BRINGS YOU LOVE

1. _____

2. _____

3. _____

4. _____

5. _____

STEP 3 - JAR OF GOOD THINGS

1. SUNRISE_____

2. MID-DAY_____

3. SUNSET _____

STEP 4 - FUTURE GOALS & VISIONS

1. _____ DESIRED EMOTION _____

2. _____ DESIRED EMOTION _____

3. _____ DESIRED EMOTION _____

STEP 5 - BECOMING YOUR IDEAL VERSION, your own HERO

Who will you be: _____

What title will you hold: _____

Who will be in your life: _____

What will your life look like:_____

What emotions will you mainly embody: _____

DAY_____ OF THE 45 DAY ABUNDANCE MINDSET ACTIVATION

WHAT ARE YOUR TRUTHS?

CONFIDENTLY state your truths and affirmations today.

I AM _____

I AM _____

I AM _____

STEP 2 - WHAT & WHO BRINGS YOU LOVE

1. _____

2. _____

3. _____

4. _____

5. _____

STEP 3 - JAR OF GOOD THINGS

1. SUNRISE_____

2. MID-DAY_____

3. SUNSET _____

STEP 4 - FUTURE GOALS & VISIONS

1. _____ DESIRED EMOTION _____

2. _____ DESIRED EMOTION _____

3. _____ DESIRED EMOTION _____

STEP 5 - BECOMING YOUR IDEAL VERSION, your own HERO

Who will you be: _____

What title will you hold: _____

Who will be in your life: _____

What will your life look like:_____

What emotions will you mainly embody: _____

DAY_____ OF THE 45 DAY ABUNDANCE MINDSET ACTIVATION

WHAT ARE YOUR TRUTHS?

CONFIDENTLY state your truths and affirmations today.

I AM _____

I AM _____

I AM _____

STEP 2 - WHAT & WHO BRINGS YOU LOVE

1. _____

2. _____

3. _____

4. _____

5. _____

STEP 3 - JAR OF GOOD THINGS

1. SUNRISE_____

2. MID-DAY_____

3. SUNSET _____

STEP 4 - FUTURE GOALS & VISIONS

1. _____ DESIRED EMOTION _____

2. _____ DESIRED EMOTION _____

3. _____ DESIRED EMOTION _____

STEP 5 - BECOMING YOUR IDEAL VERSION, your own HERO

Who will you be: _____

What title will you hold: _____

Who will be in your life: _____

What will your life look like:_____

What emotions will you mainly embody: _____

2020 © The Abundance Mindset

DAY_____ OF THE 45 DAY ABUNDANCE MINDSET ACTIVATION

WHAT ARE YOUR TRUTHS?

CONFIDENTLY state your truths and affirmations today.

I AM _____

I AM _____

I AM _____

STEP 2 - WHAT & WHO BRINGS YOU LOVE

1. _____

2. _____

3. _____

4. _____

5. _____

STEP 3 - JAR OF GOOD THINGS

1. SUNRISE _____

2. MID-DAY _____

3. SUNSET _____

STEP 4 - FUTURE GOALS & VISIONS

1. _____ DESIRED EMOTION _____

2. _____ DESIRED EMOTION _____

3. _____ DESIRED EMOTION _____

STEP 5 - BECOMING YOUR IDEAL VERSION, your own HERO

Who will you be: _____

What title will you hold: _____

Who will be in your life: _____

What will your life look like: _____

What emotions will you mainly embody: _____

DAY_____ OF THE 45 DAY ABUNDANCE MINDSET ACTIVATION

WHAT ARE YOUR TRUTHS?

CONFIDENTLY state your truths and affirmations today.

I AM _____

I AM _____

I AM _____

STEP 2 - WHAT & WHO BRINGS YOU LOVE

1. _____

2. _____

3. _____

4. _____

5. _____

STEP 3 - JAR OF GOOD THINGS

1. SUNRISE_____

2. MID-DAY_____

3. SUNSET _____

STEP 4 - FUTURE GOALS & VISIONS

1. _____ DESIRED EMOTION _____

2. _____ DESIRED EMOTION _____

3. _____ DESIRED EMOTION _____

STEP 5 - BECOMING YOUR IDEAL VERSION, your own HERO

Who will you be: _____

What title will you hold: _____

Who will be in your life: _____

What will your life look like:_____

What emotions will you mainly embody: _____

DAY_____ OF THE 45 DAY ABUNDANCE MINDSET ACTIVATION

WHAT ARE YOUR TRUTHS?

CONFIDENTLY state your truths and affirmations today.

I AM _____

I AM _____

I AM _____

STEP 2 - WHAT & WHO BRINGS YOU LOVE

1. _____

2. _____

3. _____

4. _____

5. _____

STEP 3 - JAR OF GOOD THINGS

1. SUNRISE_____

2. MID-DAY_____

3. SUNSET _____

STEP 4 - FUTURE GOALS & VISIONS

1. _____ DESIRED EMOTION _____

2. _____ DESIRED EMOTION _____

3. _____ DESIRED EMOTION _____

STEP 5 - BECOMING YOUR IDEAL VERSION, your own HERO

Who will you be: _____

What title will you hold: _____

Who will be in your life: _____

What will your life look like: _____

What emotions will you mainly embody: _____

DAY_____ OF THE 45 DAY ABUNDANCE MINDSET ACTIVATION

WHAT ARE YOUR TRUTHS?

CONFIDENTLY state your truths and affirmations today.

I AM _____

I AM _____

I AM _____

STEP 2 - WHAT & WHO BRINGS YOU LOVE

1. _____

2. _____

3. _____

4. _____

5. _____

STEP 3 - JAR OF GOOD THINGS

1. SUNRISE_____

2. MID-DAY_____

3. SUNSET _____

STEP 4 - FUTURE GOALS & VISIONS

1. _____ DESIRED EMOTION _____

2. _____ DESIRED EMOTION _____

3. _____ DESIRED EMOTION _____

STEP 5 - BECOMING YOUR IDEAL VERSION, your own HERO

Who will you be: _____

What title will you hold: _____

Who will be in your life: _____

What will your life look like:_____

What emotions will you mainly embody: _____

DAY_____ OF THE 45 DAY ABUNDANCE MINDSET ACTIVATION

WHAT ARE YOUR TRUTHS?

CONFIDENTLY state your truths and affirmations today.

I AM _____

I AM _____

I AM _____

STEP 2 - WHAT & WHO BRINGS YOU LOVE

1. _____

2. _____

3. _____

4. _____

5. _____

STEP 3 - JAR OF GOOD THINGS

1. SUNRISE_____

2. MID-DAY_____

3. SUNSET _____

STEP 4 - FUTURE GOALS & VISIONS

1. _____ DESIRED EMOTION _____

2. _____ DESIRED EMOTION _____

3. _____ DESIRED EMOTION _____

STEP 5 - BECOMING YOUR IDEAL VERSION, your own HERO

Who will you be: _____

What title will you hold: _____

Who will be in your life: _____

What will your life look like:_____

What emotions will you mainly embody: _____

DAY_____ OF THE 45 DAY ABUNDANCE MINDSET ACTIVATION

WHAT ARE YOUR TRUTHS?

CONFIDENTLY state your truths and affirmations today.

I AM _____

I AM _____

I AM _____

STEP 2 - WHAT & WHO BRINGS YOU LOVE

1. _____

2. _____

3. _____

4. _____

5. _____

STEP 3 - JAR OF GOOD THINGS

1. SUNRISE_____

2. MID-DAY_____

3. SUNSET _____

STEP 4 - FUTURE GOALS & VISIONS

1. _____ DESIRED EMOTION _____

2. _____ DESIRED EMOTION _____

3. _____ DESIRED EMOTION _____

STEP 5 - BECOMING YOUR IDEAL VERSION, your own HERO

Who will you be: _____

What title will you hold: _____

Who will be in your life: _____

What will your life look like:_____

What emotions will you mainly embody: _____

DAY_____ OF THE 45 DAY ABUNDANCE MINDSET ACTIVATION

WHAT ARE YOUR TRUTHS?

CONFIDENTLY state your truths and affirmations today.

I AM _____

I AM _____

I AM _____

STEP 2 - WHAT & WHO BRINGS YOU LOVE

1. _____

2. _____

3. _____

4. _____

5. _____

STEP 3 - JAR OF GOOD THINGS

1. SUNRISE_____

2. MID-DAY_____

3. SUNSET _____

STEP 4 - FUTURE GOALS & VISIONS

1. _____ DESIRED EMOTION _____

2. _____ DESIRED EMOTION _____

3. _____ DESIRED EMOTION _____

STEP 5 - BECOMING YOUR IDEAL VERSION, your own HERO

Who will you be: _____

What title will you hold: _____

Who will be in your life: _____

What will your life look like:_____

What emotions will you mainly embody: _____

DAY_____ OF THE 45 DAY ABUNDANCE MINDSET ACTIVATION

WHAT ARE YOUR TRUTHS?

CONFIDENTLY state your truths and affirmations today.

I AM _____

I AM _____

I AM _____

STEP 2 - WHAT & WHO BRINGS YOU LOVE

1. _____

2. _____

3. _____

4. _____

5. _____

STEP 3 - JAR OF GOOD THINGS

1. SUNRISE_____

2. MID-DAY_____

3. SUNSET _____

STEP 4 - FUTURE GOALS & VISIONS

1. _____ DESIRED EMOTION _____

2. _____ DESIRED EMOTION _____

3. _____ DESIRED EMOTION _____

STEP 5 - BECOMING YOUR IDEAL VERSION, your own HERO

Who will you be: _____

What title will you hold: _____

Who will be in your life: _____

What will your life look like:_____

What emotions will you mainly embody: _____

DAY_____ **OF THE 45 DAY ABUNDANCE MINDSET ACTIVATION**

WHAT ARE YOUR TRUTHS?

CONFIDENTLY state your truths and affirmations today.

I AM _____

I AM _____

I AM _____

STEP 2 - WHAT & WHO BRINGS YOU LOVE

1. _____

2. _____

3. _____

4. _____

5. _____

STEP 3 - JAR OF GOOD THINGS

1. SUNRISE_____

2. MID-DAY_____

3. SUNSET _____

STEP 4 - FUTURE GOALS & VISIONS

1. _____ DESIRED EMOTION _____

2. _____ DESIRED EMOTION _____

3. _____ DESIRED EMOTION _____

STEP 5 - BECOMING YOUR IDEAL VERSION, your own HERO

Who will you be: _____

What title will you hold: _____

Who will be in your life: _____

What will your life look like:_____

What emotions will you mainly embody: _____

DAY_____ OF THE 45 DAY ABUNDANCE MINDSET ACTIVATION

WHAT ARE YOUR TRUTHS?

CONFIDENTLY state your truths and affirmations today.

I AM _____

I AM _____

I AM _____

STEP 2 - WHAT & WHO BRINGS YOU LOVE

1. _____

2. _____

3. _____

4. _____

5. _____

STEP 3 - JAR OF GOOD THINGS

1. SUNRISE _____

2. MID-DAY _____

3. SUNSET _____

STEP 4 - FUTURE GOALS & VISIONS

1. _____ DESIRED EMOTION _____

2. _____ DESIRED EMOTION _____

3. _____ DESIRED EMOTION _____

STEP 5 - BECOMING YOUR IDEAL VERSION, your own HERO

Who will you be: _____

What title will you hold: _____

Who will be in your life: _____

What will your life look like: _____

What emotions will you mainly embody: _____

DAY_____ OF THE 45 DAY ABUNDANCE MINDSET ACTIVATION

WHAT ARE YOUR TRUTHS?

CONFIDENTLY state your truths and affirmations today.

I AM _____

I AM _____

I AM _____

STEP 2 - WHAT & WHO BRINGS YOU LOVE

1. _____

2. _____

3. _____

4. _____

5. _____

STEP 3 - JAR OF GOOD THINGS

1. SUNRISE_____

2. MID-DAY_____

3. SUNSET _____

STEP 4 - FUTURE GOALS & VISIONS

1. _____ DESIRED EMOTION _____

2. _____ DESIRED EMOTION _____

3. _____ DESIRED EMOTION _____

STEP 5 - BECOMING YOUR IDEAL VERSION, your own HERO

Who will you be: _____

What title will you hold: _____

Who will be in your life: _____

What will your life look like:_____

What emotions will you mainly embody: _____

DAY_____ OF THE 45 DAY ABUNDANCE MINDSET ACTIVATION

WHAT ARE YOUR TRUTHS?

CONFIDENTLY state your truths and affirmations today.

I AM _____

I AM _____

I AM _____

STEP 2 - WHAT & WHO BRINGS YOU LOVE

1. _____

2. _____

3. _____

4. _____

5. _____

STEP 3 - JAR OF GOOD THINGS

1. SUNRISE_____

2. MID-DAY_____

3. SUNSET _____

STEP 4 - FUTURE GOALS & VISIONS

1. _____ DESIRED EMOTION _____

2. _____ DESIRED EMOTION _____

3. _____ DESIRED EMOTION _____

STEP 5 - BECOMING YOUR IDEAL VERSION, your own HERO

Who will you be: _____

What title will you hold: _____

Who will be in your life: _____

What will your life look like:_____

What emotions will you mainly embody: _____

DAY _____ OF THE 45 DAY ABUNDANCE MINDSET ACTIVATION

WHAT ARE YOUR TRUTHS?

CONFIDENTLY state your truths and affirmations today.

I AM _____

I AM _____

I AM _____

STEP 2 - WHAT & WHO BRINGS YOU LOVE

1. _____
2. _____
3. _____
4. _____
5. _____

STEP 3 - JAR OF GOOD THINGS

1. SUNRISE _____

2. MID-DAY _____

3. SUNSET _____

STEP 4 - FUTURE GOALS & VISIONS

1. _____ DESIRED EMOTION _____

2. _____ DESIRED EMOTION _____

3. _____ DESIRED EMOTION _____

STEP 5 - BECOMING YOUR IDEAL VERSION, your own HERO

Who will you be: _____

What title will you hold: _____

Who will be in your life: _____

What will your life look like: _____

What emotions will you mainly embody: _____

DAY_____ OF THE 45 DAY ABUNDANCE MINDSET ACTIVATION

WHAT ARE YOUR TRUTHS?

CONFIDENTLY state your truths and affirmations today.

I AM _____

I AM _____

I AM _____

STEP 2 - WHAT & WHO BRINGS YOU LOVE

1. _____
2. _____
3. _____
4. _____
5. _____

STEP 3 - JAR OF GOOD THINGS

1. SUNRISE_____

2. MID-DAY_____

3. SUNSET _____

STEP 4 - FUTURE GOALS & VISIONS

1. _____ DESIRED EMOTION _____

2. _____ DESIRED EMOTION _____

3. _____ DESIRED EMOTION _____

STEP 5 - BECOMING YOUR IDEAL VERSION, your own HERO

Who will you be: _____

What title will you hold: _____

Who will be in your life: _____

What will your life look like:_____

What emotions will you mainly embody: _____

DAY_____ **OF THE 45 DAY ABUNDANCE MINDSET ACTIVATION**

WHAT ARE YOUR TRUTHS?

CONFIDENTLY state your truths and affirmations today.

I AM _____

I AM _____

I AM _____

STEP 2 - WHAT & WHO BRINGS YOU LOVE

1. _____

2. _____

3. _____

4. _____

5. _____

STEP 3 - JAR OF GOOD THINGS

1. SUNRISE_____

2. MID-DAY_____

3. SUNSET _____

STEP 4 - FUTURE GOALS & VISIONS

1. _____ DESIRED EMOTION _____

2. _____ DESIRED EMOTION _____

3. _____ DESIRED EMOTION _____

STEP 5 - BECOMING YOUR IDEAL VERSION, your own HERO

Who will you be: _____

What title will you hold: _____

Who will be in your life: _____

What will your life look like:_____

What emotions will you mainly embody: _____

DAY_____ **OF THE 45 DAY ABUNDANCE MINDSET ACTIVATION**

WHAT ARE YOUR TRUTHS?

CONFIDENTLY state your truths and affirmations today.

I AM _____

I AM _____

I AM _____

STEP 2 - WHAT & WHO BRINGS YOU LOVE

1. _____

2. _____

3. _____

4. _____

5. _____

STEP 3 - JAR OF GOOD THINGS

1. SUNRISE_____

2. MID-DAY_____

3. SUNSET _____

STEP 4 - FUTURE GOALS & VISIONS

1. _____ DESIRED EMOTION _____

2. _____ DESIRED EMOTION _____

3. _____ DESIRED EMOTION _____

STEP 5 - BECOMING YOUR IDEAL VERSION, your own HERO

Who will you be: _____

What title will you hold: _____

Who will be in your life: _____

What will your life look like:_____

What emotions will you mainly embody: _____

DAY_____ OF THE 45 DAY ABUNDANCE MINDSET ACTIVATION

WHAT ARE YOUR TRUTHS?

CONFIDENTLY state your truths and affirmations today.

I AM _____

I AM _____

I AM _____

STEP 2 - WHAT & WHO BRINGS YOU LOVE

1. _____

2. _____

3. _____

4. _____

5. _____

STEP 3 - JAR OF GOOD THINGS

1. SUNRISE_____

2. MID-DAY_____

3. SUNSET _____

STEP 4 - FUTURE GOALS & VISIONS

1. _____ DESIRED EMOTION _____

2. _____ DESIRED EMOTION _____

3. _____ DESIRED EMOTION _____

STEP 5 - BECOMING YOUR IDEAL VERSION, your own HERO

Who will you be: _____

What title will you hold: _____

Who will be in your life: _____

What will your life look like:_____

What emotions will you mainly embody: _____

DAY_____ OF THE 45 DAY ABUNDANCE MINDSET ACTIVATION

WHAT ARE YOUR TRUTHS?

CONFIDENTLY state your truths and affirmations today.

I AM _____

I AM _____

I AM _____

STEP 2 - WHAT & WHO BRINGS YOU LOVE

1. _____
2. _____
3. _____
4. _____
5. _____

STEP 3 - JAR OF GOOD THINGS

1. SUNRISE_____
2. MID-DAY_____
3. SUNSET _____

STEP 4 - FUTURE GOALS & VISIONS

1. _____ DESIRED EMOTION _____
2. _____ DESIRED EMOTION _____
3. _____ DESIRED EMOTION _____

STEP 5 - BECOMING YOUR IDEAL VERSION, your own HERO

Who will you be: _____

What title will you hold: _____

Who will be in your life: _____

What will your life look like:_____

What emotions will you mainly embody: _____

DAY_____ OF THE 45 DAY ABUNDANCE MINDSET ACTIVATION

WHAT ARE YOUR TRUTHS?

CONFIDENTLY state your truths and affirmations today.

I AM _____

I AM _____

I AM _____

STEP 2 - WHAT & WHO BRINGS YOU LOVE

1. _____

2. _____

3. _____

4. _____

5. _____

STEP 3 - JAR OF GOOD THINGS

1. SUNRISE_____

2. MID-DAY_____

3. SUNSET _____

STEP 4 - FUTURE GOALS & VISIONS

1. _____ DESIRED EMOTION _____

2. _____ DESIRED EMOTION _____

3. _____ DESIRED EMOTION _____

STEP 5 - BECOMING YOUR IDEAL VERSION, your own HERO

Who will you be: _____

What title will you hold: _____

Who will be in your life: _____

What will your life look like:_____

What emotions will you mainly embody: _____

DAY_____ **OF THE 45 DAY ABUNDANCE MINDSET ACTIVATION**

WHAT ARE YOUR TRUTHS?

CONFIDENTLY state your truths and affirmations today.

I AM _____

I AM _____

I AM _____

STEP 2 - WHAT & WHO BRINGS YOU LOVE

1. _____

2. _____

3. _____

4. _____

5. _____

STEP 3 - JAR OF GOOD THINGS

1. SUNRISE_____

2. MID-DAY_____

3. SUNSET _____

STEP 4 - FUTURE GOALS & VISIONS

1. _____ DESIRED EMOTION _____

2. _____ DESIRED EMOTION _____

3. _____ DESIRED EMOTION _____

STEP 5 - BECOMING YOUR IDEAL VERSION, your own HERO

Who will you be: _____

What title will you hold: _____

Who will be in your life: _____

What will your life look like:_____

What emotions will you mainly embody: _____

2020 © The Abundance Mindset

DAY_____ OF THE 45 DAY ABUNDANCE MINDSET ACTIVATION

WHAT ARE YOUR TRUTHS?

CONFIDENTLY state your truths and affirmations today.

I AM _____

I AM _____

I AM _____

STEP 2 - WHAT & WHO BRINGS YOU LOVE

1. _____
2. _____
3. _____
4. _____
5. _____

STEP 3 - JAR OF GOOD THINGS

1. SUNRISE_____

2. MID-DAY_____

3. SUNSET _____

STEP 4 - FUTURE GOALS & VISIONS

1. _____ DESIRED EMOTION _____

2. _____ DESIRED EMOTION _____

3. _____ DESIRED EMOTION _____

STEP 5 - BECOMING YOUR IDEAL VERSION, your own HERO

Who will you be: _____

What title will you hold: _____

Who will be in your life: _____

What will your life look like:_____

What emotions will you mainly embody: _____

DAY_____ **OF THE 45 DAY ABUNDANCE MINDSET ACTIVATION**

WHAT ARE YOUR TRUTHS?

CONFIDENTLY state your truths and affirmations today.

I AM _____

I AM _____

I AM _____

STEP 2 - WHAT & WHO BRINGS YOU LOVE

1. _____

2. _____

3. _____

4. _____

5. _____

STEP 3 - JAR OF GOOD THINGS

1. SUNRISE_____

2. MID-DAY_____

3. SUNSET _____

STEP 4 - FUTURE GOALS & VISIONS

1. _____ DESIRED EMOTION _____

2. _____ DESIRED EMOTION _____

3. _____ DESIRED EMOTION _____

STEP 5 - BECOMING YOUR IDEAL VERSION, your own HERO

Who will you be: _____

What title will you hold: _____

Who will be in your life: _____

What will your life look like:_____

What emotions will you mainly embody: _____

DAY_____ OF THE 45 DAY ABUNDANCE MINDSET ACTIVATION

WHAT ARE YOUR TRUTHS?

CONFIDENTLY state your truths and affirmations today.

I AM _____

I AM _____

I AM _____

STEP 2 - WHAT & WHO BRINGS YOU LOVE

1. _____

2. _____

3. _____

4. _____

5. _____

STEP 3 - JAR OF GOOD THINGS

1. SUNRISE_____

2. MID-DAY_____

3. SUNSET _____

STEP 4 - FUTURE GOALS & VISIONS

1. _____ DESIRED EMOTION _____

2. _____ DESIRED EMOTION _____

3. _____ DESIRED EMOTION _____

STEP 5 - BECOMING YOUR IDEAL VERSION, your own HERO

Who will you be: _____

What title will you hold: _____

Who will be in your life: _____

What will your life look like:_____

What emotions will you mainly embody: _____

DAY_____ OF THE 45 DAY ABUNDANCE MINDSET ACTIVATION

WHAT ARE YOUR TRUTHS?

CONFIDENTLY state your truths and affirmations today.

I AM _____

I AM _____

I AM _____

STEP 2 - WHAT & WHO BRINGS YOU LOVE

1. _____

2. _____

3. _____

4. _____

5. _____

STEP 3 - JAR OF GOOD THINGS

1. SUNRISE_____

2. MID-DAY_____

3. SUNSET _____

STEP 4 - FUTURE GOALS & VISIONS

1. _____ DESIRED EMOTION _____

2. _____ DESIRED EMOTION _____

3. _____ DESIRED EMOTION _____

STEP 5 - BECOMING YOUR IDEAL VERSION, your own HERO

Who will you be: _____

What title will you hold: _____

Who will be in your life: _____

What will your life look like:_____

What emotions will you mainly embody: _____

DAY_____ OF THE 45 DAY ABUNDANCE MINDSET ACTIVATION

WHAT ARE YOUR TRUTHS?

CONFIDENTLY state your truths and affirmations today.

I AM _____

I AM _____

I AM _____

STEP 2 - WHAT & WHO BRINGS YOU LOVE

1. _____

2. _____

3. _____

4. _____

5. _____

STEP 3 - JAR OF GOOD THINGS

1. SUNRISE_____

2. MID-DAY_____

3. SUNSET _____

STEP 4 - FUTURE GOALS & VISIONS

1. _____ DESIRED EMOTION _____

2. _____ DESIRED EMOTION _____

3. _____ DESIRED EMOTION _____

STEP 5 - BECOMING YOUR IDEAL VERSION, your own HERO

Who will you be: _____

What title will you hold: _____

Who will be in your life: _____

What will your life look like:_____

What emotions will you mainly embody: _____

DAY_____ OF THE 45 DAY ABUNDANCE MINDSET ACTIVATION

WHAT ARE YOUR TRUTHS?

CONFIDENTLY state your truths and affirmations today.

I AM _____

I AM _____

I AM _____

STEP 2 - WHAT & WHO BRINGS YOU LOVE

1. _____
2. _____
3. _____
4. _____
5. _____

STEP 3 - JAR OF GOOD THINGS

1. SUNRISE_____

2. MID-DAY_____

3. SUNSET _____

STEP 4 - FUTURE GOALS & VISIONS

1. _____ DESIRED EMOTION _____

2. _____ DESIRED EMOTION _____

3. _____ DESIRED EMOTION _____

STEP 5 - BECOMING YOUR IDEAL VERSION, your own HERO

Who will you be: _____

What title will you hold: _____

Who will be in your life: _____

What will your life look like:_____

What emotions will you mainly embody: _____

DAY_____ OF THE 45 DAY ABUNDANCE MINDSET ACTIVATION

WHAT ARE YOUR TRUTHS?

CONFIDENTLY state your truths and affirmations today.

I AM _____

I AM _____

I AM _____

STEP 2 - WHAT & WHO BRINGS YOU LOVE

1. _____

2. _____

3. _____

4. _____

5. _____

STEP 3 - JAR OF GOOD THINGS

1. SUNRISE_____

2. MID-DAY_____

3. SUNSET _____

STEP 4 - FUTURE GOALS & VISIONS

1. _____ DESIRED EMOTION _____

2. _____ DESIRED EMOTION _____

3. _____ DESIRED EMOTION _____

STEP 5 - BECOMING YOUR IDEAL VERSION, your own HERO

Who will you be: _____

What title will you hold: _____

Who will be in your life: _____

What will your life look like:_____

What emotions will you mainly embody: _____

DAY_____ OF THE 45 DAY ABUNDANCE MINDSET ACTIVATION

WHAT ARE YOUR TRUTHS?

CONFIDENTLY state your truths and affirmations today.

I AM _____

I AM _____

I AM _____

STEP 2 - WHAT & WHO BRINGS YOU LOVE

1. _____

2. _____

3. _____

4. _____

5. _____

STEP 3 - JAR OF GOOD THINGS

1. SUNRISE_____

2. MID-DAY_____

3. SUNSET _____

STEP 4 - FUTURE GOALS & VISIONS

1. _____ DESIRED EMOTION _____

2. _____ DESIRED EMOTION _____

3. _____ DESIRED EMOTION _____

STEP 5 - BECOMING YOUR IDEAL VERSION, your own HERO

Who will you be: _____

What title will you hold: _____

Who will be in your life: _____

What will your life look like:_____

What emotions will you mainly embody: _____

DAY_____ OF THE 45 DAY ABUNDANCE MINDSET ACTIVATION

WHAT ARE YOUR TRUTHS?

CONFIDENTLY state your truths and affirmations today.

I AM _____

I AM _____

I AM _____

STEP 2 - WHAT & WHO BRINGS YOU LOVE

1. _____

2. _____

3. _____

4. _____

5. _____

STEP 3 - JAR OF GOOD THINGS

1. SUNRISE_____

2. MID-DAY_____

3. SUNSET _____

STEP 4 - FUTURE GOALS & VISIONS

1. _____ DESIRED EMOTION _____

2. _____ DESIRED EMOTION _____

3. _____ DESIRED EMOTION _____

STEP 5 - BECOMING YOUR IDEAL VERSION, your own HERO

Who will you be: _____

What title will you hold: _____

Who will be in your life: _____

What will your life look like:_____

What emotions will you mainly embody: _____

DAY_____ OF THE 45 DAY ABUNDANCE MINDSET ACTIVATION

WHAT ARE YOUR TRUTHS?

CONFIDENTLY state your truths and affirmations today.

I AM _____

I AM _____

I AM _____

STEP 2 - WHAT & WHO BRINGS YOU LOVE

1. _____

2. _____

3. _____

4. _____

5. _____

STEP 3 - JAR OF GOOD THINGS

1. SUNRISE_____

2. MID-DAY_____

3. SUNSET _____

STEP 4 - FUTURE GOALS & VISIONS

1. _____ DESIRED EMOTION _____

2. _____ DESIRED EMOTION _____

3. _____ DESIRED EMOTION _____

STEP 5 - BECOMING YOUR IDEAL VERSION, your own HERO

Who will you be: _____

What title will you hold: ___·_____

Who will be in your life: _____

What will your life look like:_____

What emotions will you mainly embody: _____

DAY_____ OF THE 45 DAY ABUNDANCE MINDSET ACTIVATION

WHAT ARE YOUR TRUTHS?

CONFIDENTLY state your truths and affirmations today.

I AM _____

I AM _____

I AM _____

STEP 2 - WHAT & WHO BRINGS YOU LOVE

1. _____
2. _____
3. _____
4. _____
5. _____

STEP 3 - JAR OF GOOD THINGS

1. SUNRISE_____

2. MID-DAY_____

3. SUNSET _____

STEP 4 - FUTURE GOALS & VISIONS

1. _____ DESIRED EMOTION _____

2. _____ DESIRED EMOTION _____

3. _____ DESIRED EMOTION _____

STEP 5 - BECOMING YOUR IDEAL VERSION, your own HERO

Who will you be: _____

What title will you hold: _____

Who will be in your life: _____

What will your life look like:_____

What emotions will you mainly embody: _____

DAY_____ **OF THE 45 DAY ABUNDANCE MINDSET ACTIVATION**

WHAT ARE YOUR TRUTHS?

CONFIDENTLY state your truths and affirmations today.

I AM _____

I AM _____

I AM _____

STEP 2 - WHAT & WHO BRINGS YOU LOVE

1. _____

2. _____

3. _____

4. _____

5. _____

STEP 3 - JAR OF GOOD THINGS

1. SUNRISE_____

2. MID-DAY_____

3. SUNSET _____

STEP 4 - FUTURE GOALS & VISIONS

1. _____ DESIRED EMOTION _____

2. _____ DESIRED EMOTION _____

3. _____ DESIRED EMOTION _____

STEP 5 - BECOMING YOUR IDEAL VERSION, your own HERO

Who will you be: _____

What title will you hold: _____

Who will be in your life: _____

What will your life look like:_____

What emotions will you mainly embody: _____

DAY_____ OF THE 45 DAY ABUNDANCE MINDSET ACTIVATION

WHAT ARE YOUR TRUTHS?

CONFIDENTLY state your truths and affirmations today.

I AM _____

I AM _____

I AM _____

STEP 2 - WHAT & WHO BRINGS YOU LOVE

1. _____

2. _____

3. _____

4. _____

5. _____

STEP 3 - JAR OF GOOD THINGS

1. SUNRISE_____

2. MID-DAY_____

3. SUNSET _____

STEP 4 - FUTURE GOALS & VISIONS

1. _____ DESIRED EMOTION _____

2. _____ DESIRED EMOTION _____

3. _____ DESIRED EMOTION _____

STEP 5 - BECOMING YOUR IDEAL VERSION, your own HERO

Who will you be: _____

What title will you hold: _____

Who will be in your life: _____

What will your life look like:_____

What emotions will you mainly embody: _____

DAY_____ OF THE 45 DAY ABUNDANCE MINDSET ACTIVATION

WHAT ARE YOUR TRUTHS?

CONFIDENTLY state your truths and affirmations today.

I AM _____

I AM _____

I AM _____

STEP 2 - WHAT & WHO BRINGS YOU LOVE

1. _____

2. _____

3. _____

4. _____

5. _____

STEP 3 - JAR OF GOOD THINGS

1. SUNRISE_____

2. MID-DAY_____

3. SUNSET _____

STEP 4 - FUTURE GOALS & VISIONS

1. _____ DESIRED EMOTION _____

2. _____ DESIRED EMOTION _____

3. _____ DESIRED EMOTION _____

STEP 5 - BECOMING YOUR IDEAL VERSION, your own HERO

Who will you be: _____

What title will you hold: _____

Who will be in your life: _____

What will your life look like:_____

What emotions will you mainly embody: _____

DAY_____ OF THE 45 DAY ABUNDANCE MINDSET ACTIVATION

WHAT ARE YOUR TRUTHS?

CONFIDENTLY state your truths and affirmations today.

I AM _____

I AM _____

I AM _____

STEP 2 - WHAT & WHO BRINGS YOU LOVE

1. _____

2. _____

3. _____

4. _____

5. _____

STEP 3 - JAR OF GOOD THINGS

1. SUNRISE_____

2. MID-DAY_____

3. SUNSET _____

STEP 4 - FUTURE GOALS & VISIONS

1. _____ DESIRED EMOTION _____

2. _____ DESIRED EMOTION _____

3. _____ DESIRED EMOTION _____

STEP 5 - BECOMING YOUR IDEAL VERSION, your own HERO

Who will you be: _____

What title will you hold: _____

Who will be in your life: _____

What will your life look like:_____

What emotions will you mainly embody: _____

DAY_____ OF THE 45 DAY ABUNDANCE MINDSET ACTIVATION

WHAT ARE YOUR TRUTHS?

CONFIDENTLY state your truths and affirmations today.

I AM _____

I AM _____

I AM _____

STEP 2 - WHAT & WHO BRINGS YOU LOVE

1. _____

2. _____

3. _____

4. _____

5. _____

STEP 3 - JAR OF GOOD THINGS

1. SUNRISE_____

2. MID-DAY_____

3. SUNSET _____

STEP 4 - FUTURE GOALS & VISIONS

1. _____ DESIRED EMOTION _____

2. _____ DESIRED EMOTION _____

3. _____ DESIRED EMOTION _____

STEP 5 - BECOMING YOUR IDEAL VERSION, your own HERO

Who will you be: _____

What title will you hold: _____

Who will be in your life: _____

What will your life look like:_____

What emotions will you mainly embody: _____

DAY_____ OF THE 45 DAY ABUNDANCE MINDSET ACTIVATION

WHAT ARE YOUR TRUTHS?

CONFIDENTLY state your truths and affirmations today.

I AM _____

I AM _____

I AM _____

STEP 2 - WHAT & WHO BRINGS YOU LOVE

1. _____

2. _____

3. _____

4. _____

5. _____

STEP 3 - JAR OF GOOD THINGS

1. SUNRISE _____

2. MID-DAY _____

3. SUNSET _____

STEP 4 - FUTURE GOALS & VISIONS

1. _____ DESIRED EMOTION _____

2. _____ DESIRED EMOTION _____

3. _____ DESIRED EMOTION _____

STEP 5 - BECOMING YOUR IDEAL VERSION, your own HERO

Who will you be: _____

What title will you hold: _____

Who will be in your life: _____

What will your life look like: _____

What emotions will you mainly embody: _____

DAY_____ **OF THE 45 DAY ABUNDANCE MINDSET ACTIVATION**

WHAT ARE YOUR TRUTHS?

CONFIDENTLY state your truths and affirmations today.

I AM _____

I AM _____

I AM _____

STEP 2 - WHAT & WHO BRINGS YOU LOVE

1. _____
2. _____
3. _____
4. _____
5. _____

STEP 3 - JAR OF GOOD THINGS

1. SUNRISE_____
2. MID-DAY_____
3. SUNSET _____

STEP 4 - FUTURE GOALS & VISIONS

1. _____ DESIRED EMOTION _____
2. _____ DESIRED EMOTION _____
3. _____ DESIRED EMOTION _____

STEP 5 - BECOMING YOUR IDEAL VERSION, your own HERO

Who will you be: _____

What title will you hold: _____

Who will be in your life: _____

What will your life look like:_____

What emotions will you mainly embody: _____

DAY_____ **OF THE 45 DAY ABUNDANCE MINDSET ACTIVATION**

WHAT ARE YOUR TRUTHS?

CONFIDENTLY state your truths and affirmations today.

I AM _____

I AM _____

I AM _____

STEP 2 - WHAT & WHO BRINGS YOU LOVE

1. _____
2. _____
3. _____
4. _____
5. _____

STEP 3 - JAR OF GOOD THINGS

1. SUNRISE_____

2. MID-DAY_____

3. SUNSET _____

STEP 4 - FUTURE GOALS & VISIONS

1. _____ DESIRED EMOTION _____

2. _____ DESIRED EMOTION _____

3. _____ DESIRED EMOTION _____

STEP 5 - BECOMING YOUR IDEAL VERSION, your own HERO

Who will you be: _____

What title will you hold: _____

Who will be in your life: _____

What will your life look like:_____

What emotions will you mainly embody: _____

DAY_____ **OF THE 45 DAY ABUNDANCE MINDSET ACTIVATION**

WHAT ARE YOUR TRUTHS?

CONFIDENTLY state your truths and affirmations today.

I AM _____

I AM _____

I AM _____

STEP 2 - WHAT & WHO BRINGS YOU LOVE

1. _____

2. _____

3. _____

4. _____

5. _____

STEP 3 - JAR OF GOOD THINGS

1. SUNRISE_____

2. MID-DAY_____

3. SUNSET _____

STEP 4 - FUTURE GOALS & VISIONS

1. _____ DESIRED EMOTION _____

2. _____ DESIRED EMOTION _____

3. _____ DESIRED EMOTION _____

STEP 5 - BECOMING YOUR IDEAL VERSION, your own HERO

Who will you be: _____

What title will you hold: _____

Who will be in your life: _____

What will your life look like:_____

What emotions will you mainly embody: _____